GREAT MINECRAFT® BUILDS

YOUR UNOFFICIAL GUIDE TO
BUILDING COOL
MINECRAFT®
BRIDGES

S. D. MORISON

Please visit our website, www.enslow.com. For a free color catalog of all our high-quality books, call toll free 1-800-398-2504 or fax 1-877-980-4454.

Library of Congress Cataloging-in-Publication Data
Names: Morison, S. D., author.
Title: Your unofficial guide to building cool Minecraft® bridges / S. D. Morison.
Description: New York : Enslow Publishing, [2023] | Series: Great Minecraft builds | Includes index.
Identifiers: LCCN 2022001341 (print) | LCCN 2022001342 (ebook) | ISBN 9781978529236 (set) | ISBN 9781978529243 (library binding) | ISBN 9781978529229 (paperback) | ISBN 9781978529250 (ebook)
Subjects: LCSH: Minecraft (Game)--Juvenile literature. | Bridges--Design and construction--Juvenile literature. | Building--Juvenile literature.
Classification: LCC GV1469.35.M535 M67 2023 (print) | LCC GV1469.35.M535 (ebook) | DDC 794.8/5--dc23
LC record available at https://lccn.loc.gov/2022001341
LC ebook record available at https://lccn.loc.gov/2022001342

Published in 2023 by
Enslow Publishing
29 E. 21st Street
New York, NY 10010

Copyright © 2023 Enslow Publishing

Portions of this work were originally authored by Ryan Nagelhout and published as *The Unofficial Guide to Building Bridges in Minecraft*. All new material this edition authored by S. D. Morison.

Designer: Rachel Rising
Editor: Jill Keppeler
Illustrator: Matías Lapegüe

Photo credits: Cover, pp. 1-4, 6, 8, 10, 12, 14, 16, 18, 20, 22-24 Orange Sky ART/Shutterstock.com; Cover, pp. 1-24 Phoenix 1319/Shutterstock.com; Cover, 1, 3, 6, 8, 10, 14 18, 22-24 Soloma/Shutterstock.com; p. 4 Mihai_Andritoiu/Shutterstock.com; pp. 6, 8, 10, 14, 18 Phoenix 1319/Shutterstock.com; p. 7 Preecha Buathong/Shutterstock.com; p. 12 alanf/Shutterstock.com; p. 13 A7880S/Shutterstock.com; p. 16 Richie Chan/Shutterstock.com

Printed in the United States of America

Some of the images in this book illustrate individuals who are models. The depictions do not imply actual situations or events.

CPSIA compliance information: Batch #CSENS23: For further information contact Enslow Publishing, New York, New York, at 1-800-398-2504.

Find us on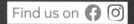

CONTENTS

Anything You Want 4

Why Build a Bridge? 6

All About the Blocks 8

Choosing a Site 10

Arches, Beams,
  and Cables 12

Starting Out 14

Side by Side 16

Moats and More 18

Bridge the Gap 20

Glossary 22

For More Information 23

Index 24

Words in the glossary appear in **bold** type
the first time they are used in the text.

ANYTHING YOU WANT

In the real world, people who **design** and build bridges need to worry about forces such as **gravity**. But this isn't (always) true in *Minecraft*! In this sandbox game, as long as you collect the **materials**, you can build anything you want. You can build amazing fantasy bridges or simple block bridges. It's all up to you.

Although you don't need to worry about as many natural forces to build bridges in *Minecraft*, learning more about **engineering** and **technology** can help you make your bridges look even better. The most important thing, though, is your imagination!

In *Minecraft*, it's fairly easy to splash across even big areas of water. A bridge can make things easier, though—and it can look really cool!

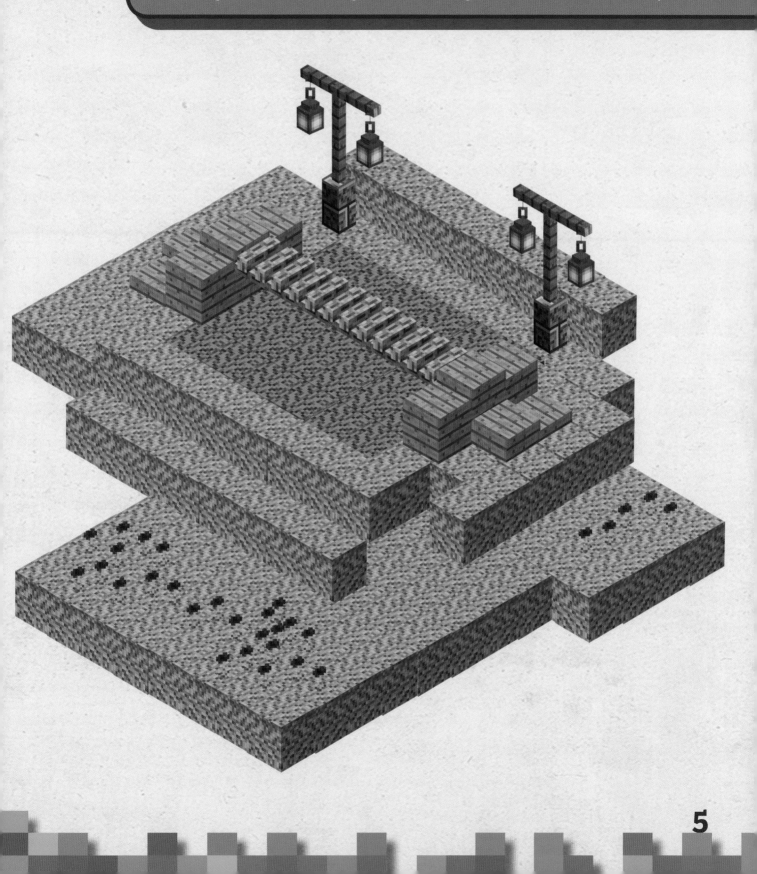

WHY BUILD A BRIDGE?

Humans started making bridges a long time ago. They needed them to cross areas (such as rivers or valleys) that were otherwise hard to cross. The first bridges were probably stepping-stones or fallen trees. You can make simple bridges like this in *Minecraft* too.

However, if you want a fancier bridge, you can do that! Bridges have two main parts, including a **span** that crosses the gap you want to bridge and supports that hold the span up. In *Minecraft*, you don't need to have supports, but they can make your bridge look better.

ADVENTURE MODE

Most blocks in *Minecraft* aren't affected by gravity. You can stack them and take out supports and they won't fall. However, sand, gravel, and a few others are affected by gravity.

Your *Minecraft* bridges can be big and fancy or just a one-block-wide row of cobblestone. It's all about what you want to build.

ALL ABOUT THE BLOCKS

Just about everything in *Minecraft* is made of blocks: blocks of dirt, blocks of stone, blocks of ore. Some, like stone, dirt, and wood, are very plain. Some, like obsidian and iron, are very tough. And some, like gold and amethyst, are fancy and shining!

You can collect *Minecraft* blocks in different ways. You can dig up dirt and chop down trees for wood. You can mine ores and different kinds of stone. More unusual kinds of blocks, such as quartz and prismarine, are only found in certain places. You'll have to hunt for them!

ADVENTURE MODE

One of the strongest (and hardest to create) blocks in *Minecraft* is a netherite block. You need eight netherite **ingots** to make one, though, and you need **ancient debris** to make netherite. It's very hard to find!

LEAVES

STONE

Each block in *Minecraft* has a blast resistance, which is how much it stands up to **explosions** caused by a creeper or TNT. The most common blocks tend to have a lower blast resistance.

DIRT

WOOD

GRASS

CHOOSING A SITE

Picking a place for a *Minecraft* bridge can be as easy as knowing where you need one! Maybe you need to cross some water or a pool of lava. Maybe you want to get from hilltop to hilltop without climbing down into a valley and then back up the next hill.

First, figure out how long the span will have to be. Then, figure out how wide the bridge should be and if you want any extras, such as supports. Collect all the materials you need before you start building.

ADVENTURE MODE

Don't use wood or wool blocks when building around or over lava. They can catch on fire! Stone will not.

You can use fences made of wood, bricks, or many kinds of stone to add railings to your bridge.

ARCHES, BEAMS, AND CABLES

Minecraft bridges can be as unusual as you want them to be. You can build one out of emerald or amethyst—or ice! You can have one that soars between mountaintops in the clouds with no supports.

However, there are types of real bridges you can build too. A beam bridge is just a straight span over the water with supports underneath. An arch bridge has supports that arc up to the span to support its weight. Suspension bridges have cables above the span to help suspend, or keep up, the weight.

There are many kinds of bridges. You can combine types with unusual *Minecraft* building materials to make a **unique** bridge!

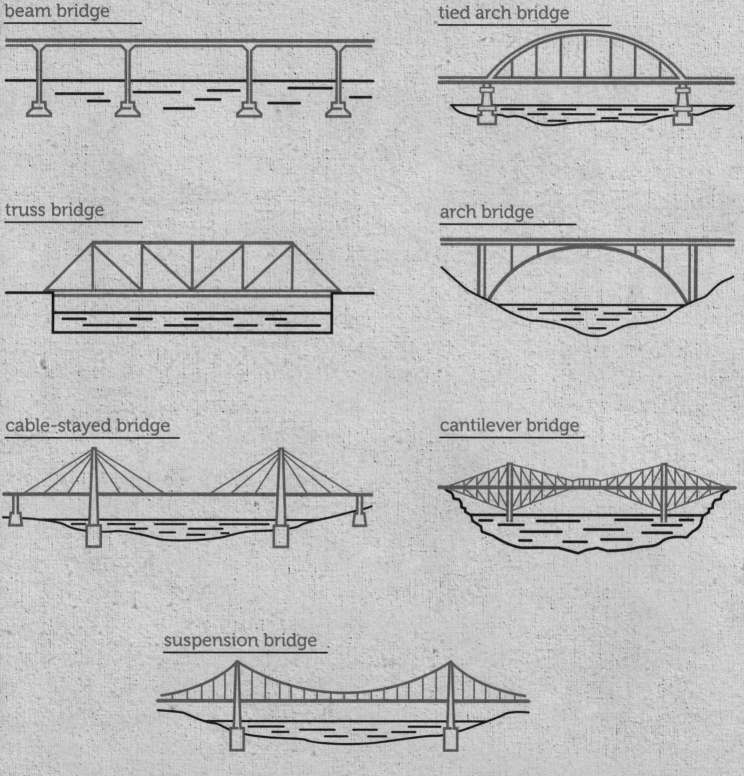

beam bridge

tied arch bridge

truss bridge

arch bridge

cable-stayed bridge

cantilever bridge

suspension bridge

STARTING OUT

If you want, you can start one or both of the sides of your bridge with stairs to lift the span a little. Many blocks in *Minecraft* have a matching stair block. You can use six blocks of the regular materials to make four stair blocks. You could also build an entrance for your bridge, such as an archway.

Once you're at the part of your bridge you want to be flat, you can "sneak" to keep yourself from falling. This also helps you see the end of the last block you set at your feet.

ADVENTURE MODE

In *Minecraft*'s creative mode, you can fly, so you don't have to worry about falling as you build your bridge. You also get an endless supply of blocks.

Minecraft brick blocks can make interesting bridges, but they take some effort. You have to dig up clay from *Minecraft* rivers and lakes, bake it in a furnace, and then combine it for a block!

SIDE BY SIDE

You might want your *Minecraft* bridge to be symmetrical. This means it has the same number of blocks on each side. This can help make your build look great. It can also make it easier to mark the middle to add a tower or another special feature.

If you want something different, though, that's OK. Maybe you want your bridge to be very steep on one side with a more gradual slope on the other side. Or maybe you want a tall wall on one side and a clear view on the other. Go for it!

TOWER BRIDGE

If you have archways or towers on a bridge, be sure to give yourself enough room to pass underneath. Make the space at least three blocks tall to give yourself space if you're riding a horse!

MOATS AND MORE

Castles and fortresses can be common *Minecraft* builds. Bridges can work well with these. You could build your own castle on a mountain peak and add a bridge as the only way to get to it. You could also dig a moat, which is a deep, wide channel that runs around your castle, and then fill it with water or lava.

You could also use redstone to make a powered bridge. This material is mined out of redstone ore. It allows you to use switches and other special blocks that it powers.

ADVENTURE MODE

There are a few places in *Minecraft* worlds where bridges **spawn** naturally. These include Nether fortresses and **bastion remnants**, both in the Nether, and End ships, found in the End.

You could use redstone to make a bridge that allows you to hide the entrance or keep people out.

BRIDGE THE GAP

A safe bridge in *Minecraft* needs to be wide enough for your character to walk along. If you're playing in survival mode with monsters, you also need to make sure your bridge has enough light that monsters can't spawn on it! You can use lanterns or torches for this.

Beyond that, the sky's the limit. You can make small bridges that simply cross a stream. You can make huge bridges that have many decorations and span mountains. The only question is what you want to build—and what you can imagine.

What kind of bridge do you want to build? It's up to you!

21

GLOSSARY

ancient debris In *Minecraft*, a rare ore found only in the Nether. It's used with gold to make netherite.

bastion remnant In *Minecraft*, a castle-like structure only found in the Nether.

design To create the pattern or shape of something. Also, the pattern or shape of something.

engineering The use of science and math to build better objects.

explosion A sudden release of energy.

gravity The force that pulls objects toward the center of a planet or star. The force that pulls objects toward Earth's center.

ingot A piece of metal formed into a shape, such as a brick.

material Matter from which something is made.

span The part of a bridge that stretches over a length and is supported by the rest of the bridge.

spawn In a video game, to appear or cause something to appear.

technology Using science, engineering, and other industries to invent useful tools or to solve problems.

unique One of a kind.

FOR MORE INFORMATION

BOOKS

Miller, Megan. *Minecrafter Architect: The Builder's Idea Book*. New York, NY: Sky Pony Press, 2019.

Mojang AB. *Minecraft: Guide to Redstone*. London: Dean, 2021.

Swanson, Jennifer. *Bridges! With 25 Science Projects for Kids*. White River Junction, VT: Nomad Press, 2018.

WEBSITES

The Best Minecraft Builds
www.pcgamer.com/best-minecraft-builds/
Take a look at some of the amazing things people have built in *Minecraft*.

Minecraft Wiki
minecraft.fandom.com/wiki/Minecraft_Wiki
You can find information on every *Minecraft* block and mob here, as well as pictures and tutorials.

Welcome to Minecraft
www.minecraft.net/en-us
The official *Minecraft* site offers many resources.

INDEX

A
arch bridge, 12, 13
archway, 14, 17

B
beam bridge, 12, 13
blast resistance, 9

C
creative mode, 14

F
fences, 10

G
gravity, 4, 6

L
lava, 10, 18

M
moat, 18

R
redstone, 18, 19
rivers, 6, 15

S
sand, 6
span, 6, 10, 12, 14
stairs, 14
stone, 6, 7, 8, 9, 10, 11
supports, 6, 10, 12
survival mode, 20
suspension bridge, 12, 13

T
tower, 16, 17

V
valleys, 6, 10

W
water, 5, 10, 12, 18
wood, 8, 9, 10, 11